JEANLOUP SIEFF

JEANLOUP SIEFF

Erotische Photographie
Erotic Photography
Photographie érotique

Benedikt Taschen

UMSCHLAGVORDERSEITE/FRONT COVER/COUVERTURE:
Mieder/Corset, New York 1962

UMSCHLAGRÜCKSEITE/BACK COVER/AU DOS:
Frau unter einem Auto, offene Haube/Woman under a car,
bonnet up/Seule sous une voiture, capots ouverts, Paris 1975

FRONTISPIZ/FRONTISPIECE/FRONTISPICE:
Werbephoto für Strümpfe/Advertisement for stockings/Publicité
pour des collants, Paris 1988

Über Erotik

Es gibt Menschen, die ihre Erotik leben wie manch ein Heiliger seinen Glauben – leidend; andere leben sie freudig und unbekümmert, ohne sich die Fragen zu stellen, die für ihre Lust tödlich wären. Für die ersteren besteht das Leben nur durch und für den Tod; symbolisch für diesen mystischen Glauben steht die Erotik, die lustvoll zu befriedigen zur Selbstzerstörung führt.

Die Liste derer ist lang, die ihre Erotik voller Schmerz und Scham über eine Lust lebten, die sie als tödlich erkannten; sie reicht von Charles Baudelaire bis zu Georges Bataille.

Ein Humorist hat einmal gesagt: »Pornographie ist die Erotik der anderen«, und doch ist die Erotik eines jeden der geheime Garten, der den Menschen zum einzigen Lebewesen macht, das sich der Vergänglichkeit seiner Lebenslust bewußt wird.

Lebenstrieb? Todestrieb? Vermutlich beides zugleich. Übrig bleibt, daß die Erotik uns ebenso einzigartig macht, wie es unsere Fingerabdrücke tun. Und wenn es einen Bereich gibt, in dem jeder allein ist, dann gewiß den der Lust und der Phantasie, die in uns die vitalen Reflexe des ursprünglichen Verlangens erzeugen.

Alle Darstellungen des menschlichen Körpers – sei es in der Photographie oder in der Malerei – sind ebenso durch den Voyeurismus eines privilegierten Augenblicks geprägt wie durch das unreflektierte Bedürfnis, diesen festzuhalten. Jedes Bild sagt uns: »Das wird nicht mehr sein«, und zugleich sagt es: »Aber es war.«

Meine Bilder sind imaginäre Erinnerungen, in einem durchsichtigen Spiegel gesehen. Was ist jenseits des Spiegels? Ein anderer Spiegel vermutlich, der uns zu anderen Bildern führt. Kann man wie Alice die Spiegel

Eroticism

There are those who live their eroticism the way some saints lived their faith – with pain and suffering. Others live it with joy and lightheartedness, without stopping to ask questions which would destroy their pleasure. For the first group, life is only lived for death and through death. For them, eroticism represents a mystical symbolism whose appeasement through pleasure brings self-destruction.

From Charles Baudelaire to George Bataille, the list is long of those who lived their eroticism in pain and shame, knowing it to be a deadly pleasure.

A humorist once said »Pornography is other people's eroticism«. The fact remains, however, that one's own eroticism is a secret garden, which makes man the only creature to be aware of the ephemeral quality of his sensual pleasure.

A life instinct? A death wish? Probably both. Our eroticism is as unique as our fingerprints and if there's one area in which we are truly alone, it is that of sensual pleasure and fantasy, creating in us, as they do, the vital impulse of original desire.

Any representation of the human body, whether photographic or pictorial, is imbued with a privileged moment of voyeurism and a simple need to conserve that moment. Each image tells us »This will never be again« and at the same time whispers »But it once was«.

My images are imaginary memories seen through a two-way mirror. What is there beyond the mirror? Another mirror perhaps which reflects back more images.

Can we, like Alice, go through the looking-glass and discover the reality of a dream or are we destined to

De l'érotisme

Il y a des gens qui vivent leur érotisme comme certains Saints leur foi, dans la souffrance. D'autres dans la joie et l'insouciance sans se poser les questions qui tueraient leur plaisir. Pour les premiers, la vie n'existe que par et pour la mort, et l'érotisme en est la symbolique mystique dont l'assouvissement dans la jouissance provoque sa propre destruction.

De Baudelaire à Bataille, la liste est longue de ceux qui vécurent leur érotisme dans la douleur et la honte d'un plaisir qu'ils savaient mortel.

»La pornographie est l'érotisme des autres« a dit un humoriste, mais il n'empêche que l'érotisme de chacun est ce jardin secret qui fait de l'homme, le seul des êtres vivants à prendre conscience de l'éphémère de sa jouissance vitale.

Pulsion de vie? Pulsion de mort? Probablement des deux à la fois. Il reste que l'érotisme nous rend aussi unique que nos empreintes digitales, et s'il est un domaine où chacun est solitaire, c'est bien celui du plaisir et des phantasmes qui créent en nous les réflexes vitaux de l'envie originelle.

Toutes les représentations du corps humain, photographiques ou picturales, sont marquées par le voyeurisme d'un moment privilégié en même temps que par le besoin irréfléchi de sa conservation. »Cela ne sera plus« nous dit chaque image, »Mais cela fut« nous répond-elle en même temps.

Mes images sont des souvenirs imaginés vus dans un miroir sans tain. Au-delà du miroir, qu'y a-t-il? Un autre miroir probablement, qui nous renvoie à d'autres images. Mais peut – on, comme Alice, pénétrer les miroirs pour découvrir les réalités du rêve, ou sommes-nous voués à cette

durchdringen, um die Wahrheit des Traums zu ergründen, oder sind wir zu dieser ewigen Suche im Schattentheater unserer Existenz verdammt? Ich weiß diese Frage nicht zu beantworten – zum Glück; denn die Antwort wäre das Ende der Reise!

Jeanloup Sieff, März 1988

search for ever in the shadow-play of our own existence? Thankfully, I cannot answer this question, for the answer would mark the end of the quest!

Jeanloup Sieff, March 1988

quête éternelle dans le théâtre d'ombres qu'est notre existence. Heureusement, je ne puis répondre à cette question, car la réponse serait la fin du voyage!

Jeanloup Sieff, Mars 1988

Photographischer Monolog

Photographic Monologue

Monologue photographique

16. November 1980: Nach zahlreichen Irrungen, vergänglichen Gewißheiten und enttäuschten Hoffnungen wird die Photographie für mich wieder zu dem, was sie immer hätte sein sollen: das Bedauern über die verrinnende Zeit und das Bedürfnis, einige Augenblicke festzuhalten. Es geht nicht um den törichten Wunsch, sie anzuhalten, oder um den naiven Glauben, eine Photographie würde zum unvergänglichen Protokoll des Geschehenen; es geht einfach um die Materialisierung bestimmter Gefühle in bestimmten Augenblicken.

Es gibt formale Empfindungen, die durch Licht- oder Raumverhältnisse hervorgerufen werden, und rein intellektuelle Emotionen. Die Photographie kann sie alle zusammenfassen und neue daraus schaffen.

Es gibt Menschen, die nur mit dem Blick in die Zukunft leben, und andere, die die Gegenwart nur bezogen auf die Vergangenheit leben. Ich gehöre zu denen, die sich gerne erinnern. Aber ich mache keine Photographien, damit etwas stellvertretend fortbesteht; nein, die Lust, Bilder zu machen, ist etwas anderes. Eine Landschaft zu photographieren ersetzt weder die Gerüche des Windes noch die körperliche Lust, Teil eines Ortes zu sein; es ist vielmehr die formale oder gefühlsmäßige Befriedigung, diesen Ort so zu rekonstruie-

16 November 1980: After much searching, many short-lived certainties and many disappointed hopes, photography has become for me what it should always have been, perhaps what it always was – the regret of seeing time go by and the need to preserve certain moments.

It is not the desperate wish to stop time nor the naive belief that a photograph becomes an eternal statement of what once was. It's rather the simple materialisation of certain emotions at certain moments.

There are formal emotions created by light and volume, others which are sentimental or sensual and inspired by other people, and some which are purely intellectual. Photography can bring them all together and from them create new ones. There are people who look only towards the future and others who live the present for the past which it will become. I belong with those who like to look back, who like to remember. But I don't take photographs merely in order to relive moments by proxy. The pleasure in creating the image lies elsewhere. Photographing a landscape cannot replace the smell of the wind nor the physical joy of the open space. There is a formal satisfaction, sometimes a sentimental one, in reconstructing the open space as I experience it, but also as I choose to experience it, by the context in which I

16 Novembre 1980: Après de nombreuses errances, des certitudes éphémères et des espoirs déçus, la photographie redevient pour moi ce qu'elle aurait toujours dû être, ce qu'elle a d'ailleurs peut-être toujours été, le regret du temps qui passe et le besoin d'en conserver quelques moments.

Non pas le désir fou de l'arrêter ou la croyance naïve qu'une photographie deviendra le constat immortel de ce qui fut, non, mais simplement la matérialisation de certaines émotions à certains moments.

Il y a des émotions formelles, faites de lumières ou de volumes, d'autres sentimentales ou sensuelles, provoquées par des gens, certaines purement intellectuelles. La photographie peut les assembler toutes, pour ensuite en créer de nouvelles.

Il est des gens qui vivent en regardant devant eux, d'autres qui ne vivent le présent qu'en fonction du passé qu'il deviendra. Je fais partie de ceux qui se retournent, qui aiment à se souvenir. Mais je ne fais pas des photographies pour revivre par procuration; non, le plaisir de faire des images est autre. Photographier un paysage ne remplace pas les odeurs du vent ni la joie physique d'appartenir à un espace, à la fois tel que je le ressens et différent par la composition dans laquelle je l'insère et le moment que je choisis.

ren, wie ich ihn empfinde, und zugleich anders durch die Komposition, in die ich ihn einfüge, und durch meine Wahl des Augenblicks. Ein Gesicht, ein Körper, ein Licht können das gleiche Gefühl und das gleiche Verlangen hervorrufen, sie zu »rekreieren«, und zwar einerseits genau so, wie sie sind, und zugleich doch anders. Das heißt das Flüchtige erfassen und es zu etwas Dauerhaftem machen oder – wenn man so will – durch den bewußten Reflex, der die Photographie ausmacht, etwas schaffen, das sich der Sprache entzieht. Man »nimmt« eine Photographie auf, man erfaßt etwas oder jemanden, jedoch so, wie man es oder ihn selbst gesehen hat. Das Sujet besteht zwar schon vor dem Photo, das es – vorübergehend – unvergänglich macht, doch die Entscheidung, in welchem Augenblick und auf welche Weise man das »isoliert« (komponiert), was man zeigen möchte, liegt bei einem selbst.

Eben das macht die Photographie so packend; sobald ein Photo aufgenommen ist, nimmt es dem Aufgenommenen sein Eigenleben, es verselbständigt sich und spricht im Betrachter eigene Gefühle an, die manchmal sogar im Widerspruch zu der Empfindung stehen, die es entstehen ließ.

Für manche ist die Photographie nur ein Mittel zum Zweck, einer protokollarischen Feststellung, einer Reflexion über die Welt. Häufig geben die Photographien dem Inhalt den Vorrang gegenüber der Form und geben sich selbst als unsichtbare, kritische Zeugen der Ereignisse, die sie anprangern oder verherrlichen.

Sie lehnen das »schöne Bild« ab und streben nur das effektive Zeugnis an. Doch wie einfach ist es, eine Photographie zum Beleg selbst für das Gegenteil dessen zu machen, was der Photograph zu belegen glaubte!

Ein Bild ist in gewisser Weise dazu verurteilt, »schön« zu sein, was auch immer es zum Thema oder Inhalt haben und wie peinlich dies auch manchem erscheinen mag. Auch die

place« it and the moment in time which I select.

A face, a body, a certain light. All these things can inspire the same emotion and the same desire to »recreate« them, both as they are and as they might be. You are seizing hold of the fleeting and making something permanent. But you could also say that it's the creation of something intangible by the conscious act of taking a photograph.

One »takes« a photograph, one captures something or someone, but one captures only what the photographer sees, even if the subject existed prior to being immortalized – temporarily – by the photograph. The photographer is the one who decides how he will »isolate«, how he will compose what he wants to show.

And that's what makes photography so taking, in both senses of the word. As soon as it is »taken«, the photo takes you, it becomes autonomous and inspires emotions which are not only peculiar to you as you look at it, but which can also be quite opposed to the emotions which gave birth to the image.

For some people, photography is only a means to an end, with the end being a statement, a discourse, a reflection of the world. They favour content over form and see themselves as the invisible, critical witnesses of that which they either denounce or glorify. They challenge the idea of the »belle image« and seek only to maximize the efficiency of their testimony. But this testimony is a fragile thing and how easy it is to make a photograph affirm the very opposite of what the author intended.

In a sense, an image has to be »beautiful« to be effective, no matter what the subject or the reason for taking it and no matter how annoying some people may find this. After all, the »Internationale« really is a beautiful song!

I sometimes wonder if photographs of landscapes or female bodies are not really more »flagrantly subversive« than images of, for example,

Un visage, un corps, une lumière pourront provoquer la même émotion et le même désir de les »recréer«, à la fois tels qu'en eux-même et autres. C'est à la fois saisir du fugitif et en faire du durable. Ou, si l'on veut, c'est créer de l'ineffable, par ce réflexe conscient qu'est la photographie.

On »prend« une photographie, on saisit quelque chose ou quelqu'un, mais on ne voit que ce que le photographe a vu, car, même si le sujet préexiste à la photo qui l'immortalisera – temporairement – on est celui qui décide du moment et de la façon dont on »isole« (compose) ce que l'on veut montrer. Et c'est ce qui rend la photographie si prenante, dans le double sens du mot, car, aussitôt »prise«, la photo vous prend vous-même en devenant autonome et en provoquant chez ceux qui la regardent des émotions qui leur seront propres et parfois même opposées à celle qui l'a fait naître.

Pour certains, la photographie n'est qu'un moyen, au service d'un discours, d'un constat, d'une réflexion sur le monde. Ils privilégient souvent le fond à la forme et se veulent les témoins invisibles et critiques des événements qu'ils dénoncent ou glorifient.

Ils récusent la »belle image« et ne recherchent que l'efficacité du témoignage.

Mais que ce témoignage est fragile, et qu'il est facile de faire dire à une photographie le contraire même de ce que croyait affirmer son auteur!

Une image est, d'une certaine façon, condamnée à être »belle« pour être efficace, quel qu'en soit le sujet ou la raison et aussi gênant que cela puisse paraître à certains. Après tout, »l'Internationale« est avant tout une belle chanson!

Je me demande parfois si la photographie d'un paysage ou d'un corps de femme n'est pas plus chargée en »subversion exemplaire« que d'autres images de guerre ou de violences, dont la multiplicité même ne provoque, à la longue, qu'acceptation résignée de la bêtise humaine.

»Internationale« ist schließlich in erster Linie ein schönes Lied!

Manchmal frage ich mich, ob die Photographie einer Landschaft oder eines Frauenkörpers nicht mehr »exemplarisch Subversives« besitzt als andere Aufnahmen – Bilder von Krieg und Gewalt –, die gerade in ihrer Vielzahl auf lange Sicht nichts anderes bewirken als ein resigniertes Hinnehmen des menschlichen Unverstandes. Natürlich liegen die Dinge so einfach nicht; aber ohne ihre formale Klarheit hätten die Photographien von Henri Cartier-Bresson oder Eugène Smith niemals diese universelle Bedeutung erlangt; ein Porträt von Boubat weckt in mir mehr Verlangen nach einer veränderten Welt als die Aufnahme eines Massengrabes oder eines Exekutionskommandos. Zugegeben, ich habe die Dinge etwas vereinfacht; doch ich glaube (oder versuche, mich davon zu überzeugen), daß Schönheit subversiv ist; daß sie oftmals eine aufstörende Wirkung hat; daß man ihr nicht traut (eine schöne Frau *kann* nur dumm sein!); kurz, daß die Narren, die ihr mit Argwohn begegnen, recht haben, denn die Schönheit provoziert sie – und schenkt ihnen keinerlei Beachtung.

Ohne die ewige und müßige Debatte über Form und Inhalt wiederaufnehmen zu wollen, möchte ich hier festhalten, daß ich der Form den Vorrang gebe, ja sie fast als Selbstzweck ansehe, und daß die besten Absichten der Welt nicht über hilflose Versuche hinauskommen, wenn sie nicht mit absoluter formaler Klarheit zum Ausdruck gebracht werden.

Warum aber mache ich überhaupt Photos? Es gelingt mir nicht, das wirklich zu begreifen. Es hat mich eines Tages gepackt, als ich fünfzehn Jahre alt war, und seitdem hat es mich nicht mehr losgelassen. Natürlich sind manche meiner Arbeiten aus rein ökonomischen Erwägungen entstanden; denn zu meinem großen Erstaunen ist die Photographie mein Beruf geworden. Ich hatte also Aufträge zu erfüllen, egal, ob ich darin

war and violence which, due to their very number, ultimately provoke nothing more than resigned acceptance of human stupidity.

Obviously it's not that simple. However, if they had not had such rigour of composition, the photographs of Henri Cartier-Bresson or Eugène Smith would never have achieved their universal value; and more than any photograph of mass graves or firing squads, it is a portrait such as that by Boubat which really makes me dream of a different world.

It's true, I'm simplifying somewhat, but what I believe (or want to believe), is that beauty, in its general sense, is subversive, disturbing, that it's not taken seriously enough (a beautiful woman must be stupid). In short, that the fools who distrust beauty are right to do so because it challenges them and denies them existence.

I don't wish to launch into the eternal and pointless debate over form versus content, but let me just say that I favour form because I see it almost as an end in itself. You can have the best of intentions, but these will be no use and remain but incompetent efforts if they are not expressed clearly and with the greatest precision.

But why do I take photographs? It's something I still can't fully comprehend. It caught my attention one day when I was fifteen years old and I've never left it since. It is of course true that I took some of my photographs for purely economic reasons. To my great amazement, photography became my profession and I therefore had to please my clients and not only myself. But that's the fate of all photographers, and even in commissioned work it is sometimes possible to invest something of oneself. But apart from those photographs, what is the common denominator of the ones which »needed« to be taken? For myself, it's primarily the »physical pleasure« which certain images inspire in me. This occurs only rarely, when the miracle happens and there's perfect harmony between

Evidemment, les choses ne sont pas si simples, mais sans leur rigueur formelle, les photographies de Henri Cartier-Bresson ou de Eugène Smith n'auraient jamais atteint leur valeur universelle, et tel portrait de Boubat me donnera une plus grande envie d'un monde différent que tel autre d'un charnier ou d'un peloton d'exécution. D'accord, je simplifie un peu, mais ce que je crois (ou ce dont j'essaie de me persuader), c'est que la beauté, dans sons sens général, est subversive, qu'elle dérange souvent, qu'on ne lui fait pas crédit (une belle femme ne peut qu'être idiote!), bref, que les imbéciles qui se méfient d'elle ont raison, car elle les provoque et les nie.

Sans reprendre l'éternel et vain débat du fond et de la forme, mettons que je privilégie la forme parce que je la considère, presque, comme une fin en soi, alors que les meilleures intentions du monde ne resteront que balbutiements si elles ne sont exprimées avec une rigueur absolue.

Mais pourquoi fais-je des photos? Je n'arrive toujours pas à le comprendre vraiment. Cela m'a pris un jour, j'avais quinze ans, et cela n'a plus cessé depuis.

Evidemment, certaines d'entre elles ont été réalisées dans un but purement économique, car, à mon grand étonnement, c'était devenu mon métier et j'avais donc des commandes à satisfaire, à défaut de toujours me satisfaire moi-même. Mais c'est là le lot de tous les photographes, et il est des travaux de commande dans lesquels on peut, parfois, se retrouver un peu soi-même.

Mais en dehors de ces photos-là, quel est le dénominateur commun de toutes les autres, de ces »besoins«? ... Je crois que c'est avant tout, pour moi, le »plaisir physique«, celui que parfois, rarement, je ressens à certaines images, lorsque le miracle s'est accompli et que tout n'est qu'harmonie entre ce que je voulais montrer, me montrer, et la réussite des moyens mis en œuvre pour y parvenir: qualité plastique, organisation des formes, ron-

immer meine eigene Erfüllung fand. Aber das ist das Los aller Photographen. Doch von diesen Arbeiten einmal abgesehen, welchen gemeinsamen Nenner haben all die anderen Photos, die aus einem inneren Bedürfnis heraus entstanden sind? Ich glaube, für mich ist es vor allem die »körperliche Lust«, die ich manchmal – selten genug – bei bestimmten Bildern verspüre, wenn das Wunder eingetreten ist und eine völlige Harmonie besteht zwischen dem, was ich zeigen – mir zeigen – wollte, und dem Erfolg, mit dem ich die Mittel, dieses Ziel zu erreichen, eingesetzt habe: plastische Qualität, formaler Aufbau, abgerundete Lichtverhältnisse, Wahl des Augenblicks…

Gute Photographien gehen über sich hinaus, sind mehr, als man von einer Photographie erwarten kann; sie haben dieses »gewisse Etwas«, kurz: Sie sind ein kleines Wunder.

Im Grunde zeichnen sich die sogenannten »großen Photographien« lediglich dadurch aus, daß ihnen dieses glückliche Zusammentreffen verschiedener Umstände häufiger begegnet ist; denn ein gutes Photo machen heißt immer auch vom Zufall profitieren: indem man das, was einem zufällig begegnet, unmittelbar erfaßt und augenblicklich umsetzt. Selbst die konstruiertesten und »bewußtesten« Bilder bedürfen eines Wunders – eines gewissen Lichtes oder einer unerwarteten Wolke, die eine beliebige Landschaft in einen privilegierten Augenblick verwandelt. Es gibt aber nun solche, die eine derartige Gelegenheit wahrnehmen, und andere, die sich stets nur abmühen. Was mich betrifft, bin ich mir nicht im klaren. Es genügt mir, ein paar Aufnahmen gemacht zu haben, die mir gefallen, und vor allem auf weitere für die Zukunft zu hoffen.

Wie sagte Oscar Wilde: »Wenn ich mich beurteile, verabscheue ich mich. Aber wenn ich mich vergleiche…« Doch das ist unwichtig; Gefallen und Mißfallen hängen zu sehr von Modeerscheinungen ab oder von den Vorstellungen, die die Menschen

what I wanted to show, to myself, and the successful use of the means used to achieve it – the type of modelling, the use of shape, the rounded quality of light, the choice of moment…

Good photographers are rare and indefinable but they all have one thing in common. This is the ability to reach beyond themselves, to be more than they could be, to have that special genius. In short, to be a little bit miraculous.

Basically, a »great« photographer is simply one to whom this happy coincidence of events has happened a great many times. You need to have luck on your side to achieve a really good photograph. You need the right moment, to recognise it as such and instantly seize upon it. Even the most elaborate image, the most »composed«, the most »aware«, needs the miracle of light which makes the portrait unforgettable, or the unexpected cloud which transforms an ordinary landscape into something special.

But not everybody recognises the moment when it presents itself — some are blessed with the ability to see it and others just toil away.

As for myself, I don't know. I'm happy to have created a few images which give me pleasure and, above all, hope to create more in the future.

As Oscar Wilde said, »If I judge myself, I loathe myself. But if I compare myself…«. This is not important, however, as whether you please or displease is much too dependent on fashion and on what people believe they know about you. Often inaccurately. »Tell me who doesn't like you and I'll tell you who you hate« – and the misunderstanding is created, for all time.

When trying to achieve a peace of mind which often evades me, I look at certain photographs by André Kertesz. Through them I find not only peace but also the desire to continue with my work. The photograph of the entrance to Piet Mondrian's studio, with one tulip in a vase (I've just discovered it was plastic, which upset me – for Mondrian, not for Kertesz!)

deur de la lumière, choix du moment…

Les bonnes photographies sont rares et indéfinissables, mais elles ont toutes un point commun, c'est d'aller au-delà d'elles-mêmes, d'être plus que ce qu'elles pourraient être, d'avoir cette »petite musique«… bref, d'être un peu miraculeuses.

Au fond, ceux que l'on appelle des »grands photographes« ne sont que ceux auxquels cet accident heureux est arrivé un plus grand nombre de fois, car faire une bonne photo, c'est toujours gagner sur le hasard. Hasard de la rencontre, de sa compréhension immédiate, de sa transcription instantanée.

Même les images les plus élaborées, les plus construites, les plus »conscientes« ont besoin du miracle d'une certaine lumière, qui rendra tel portrait inoubliable, ou du nuage inattendu qui transformera un paysage quelconque en un moment privilégié. Mais il y a ceux qui les voient, qui ont la grâce, et ceux qui besognent.

Quant à moi, je ne sais pas. Il me suffit d'avoir fait quelques images qui me plaisent et, surtout, d'espérer en quelques autres à venir.

Comme le disait Oscar Wilde: »Quand je me juge, je me déteste. Mais quand je me compare…« Mais ceci n'est pas important, plaire ou déplaire dépend trop des modes ou de ce que les gens s'imaginent, souvent à tort, de vous. »Dis-moi qui ne t'aime pas, je te dirai qui tu hais!« et le malentendu s'installe, pour toujours.

Pour retrouver une sérénité qui souvent me fait défaut, je regarde certaines photographies de André Kertesz. Et je retrouve et la paix et l'envie de faire des choses. La photographie représentant l'entrée de l'atelier de Piet Mondrian, avec une tulipe dans un vase (je viens d'apprendre qu'elle était en plastique, et cela m'a peiné, pour Mondrian, pas pour Kertesz!), me fait oublier l'existence même des gens qui m'exaspèrent, c'est tout dire! Car parmi les qualités d'une bonne photographie (ou d'une musique, ou d'un livre…) il y a la vertu essentielle

sich von einem machen. »Sage mir, wer Dich nicht mag, und ich sage Dir, wen Du haßt!« – und das Mißverständnis ist für immer entstanden.

Um innere Ausgeglichenheit zu finden, die mir oft fehlt, sehe ich mir gerne bestimmte Photographien von André Kertesz an und finde darin sowohl Ruhe als auch die Lust, etwas zu tun. Die Photographie vom Eingang zum Atelier Piet Mondrians mit der Tulpe in der Vase (ich habe kürzlich erst erfahren, daß sie aus Plastik ist; das hat mich schmerzlich berührt – für Mondrian, nicht für Kertesz!) läßt mich die Existenz selbst der Leute vergessen, die mich maßlos aufregen; das sagt alles! Denn zu den Wesensmerkmalen einer guten Photographie (oder eines Musikstückes oder eines Buches) gehört die Kraft, milde zu stimmen; nicht allein, daß man die Existenz von Dummköpfen vergißt, sondern daß man ihnen ihr Vorhandensein verzeiht. So groß ist das Maß innerer Ausgeglichenheit, zu dem man vor einem vollkommenen Werk gelangen kann!

Wenn ich mir das Warum der Dinge nicht erklären kann, so stelle ich doch ihre Existenz fest; und was das »Warum« angeht, so antworte ich wie die Kinder mit »Darum«. Denn eine Leidenschaft oder ein Bedürfnis erklärt man nicht, eben weil es sich um ein Bedürfnis handelt.

Ich betreibe keine pädagogische Photographie. Ich versuche nicht zu erklären, nicht zu zeigen; ich versuche, mich einzufühlen. Ich mag Pädagogen nicht; es ärgert mich, wenn sie zu wissen vorgeben, wo niemand etwas weiß, und Gefühle, die sie nicht empfinden können, durch Gewißheiten ersetzen, die sie beruhigen.

Ich mag Verrückte, Poeten, solche, deren Photographien Fenster zu Welten aufstoßen, die noch niemand gesehen hat. Die Menschen bei Doisneau muß es im täglichen Leben geben, er hat sie ja photographiert; aber wieso sieht nur er diese Menschen? Er ist eben begnadet.

Es gibt Leute, die Fragen mit schlagenden Argumenten begegnen, und

makes me forget the very existence of those who exasperate me. I think this says it all. Among the many qualities of a good photograph (or a good piece of music or a good book…) is the essential virtue of making one more tolerant, so that one can not only forget the existence of fools, one can actually forgive them for existing – so great is the degree of serenity which can be achieved when a work is accomplished!

If I cannot understand the »why« of things, at least I can confirm that they exist and to the »why«?, I reply, like a child, »Because!«. Because you cannot explain a passion, a need. And a need is what it is.

I don't like lessons on photograhy. I don't seek to explain, not even to show, I want only to experience. I don't like teachers. They bore me because they pretend to know what nobody knows and they do so by replacing emotions they are incapable of feeling by convictions which give reassurance.

I like madmen, poets, those whose photographs open up windows onto lights and universes never seen before. Robert Doisneau's characters probably existed in everyday life before he photographed them, why then can he alone see them? Because he is inspired.

There are those who demand and those who question. Those of the exclamation mark and those of the question mark. But what could be more beautiful, even just typographically, than a question mark? »Death and vulgarity are the only things which one cannot explain« wrote Oscar Wilde (him again!). But this is just a clever remark. Nothing can be explained, even if you spend your life trying to do so. Some people make this claim for photography – that it can explain by recording »objectively«.

What a mistake! Photography is nothing but semblance, it shows nothing. For one person a face will be sad, for another it will be bored, for a third it will be peaceful.

de rendre clément, non seulement d'oublier l'existence des imbéciles, mais de leur pardonner d'être, tel est grand le degré de sérénité que l'on eut atteindre devant une œuvre accomplie! Si je ne peux expliquer le pourquoi des choses, du moins j'en constate l'existence, et à »pourquoi?«, je réponds, comme les enfants, »parce que!« Parce qu'on n'explique pas une passion, un besoin, car c'est bien d'un »besoin« qu'il s'agit.

Je n'aime pas la photographie pédagogique. Je ne cherche pas à expliquer, même pas à montrer, je cherche tout au plus à ressentir. Je n'aime pas les pédagogues, ils m'ennuient en prétendant savoir, quand personne ne sait. Ils remplacent les émotions qu'ils ne peuvent éprouver par des certitudes qui les rassurent.

J'aime les fous, les poètes, ceux dont les photographies ouvrent des fenêtres sur des lumières et des univers jamais vus par d'autres. Les personnages de Doisneau doivent bien exister dans la vie courante puisqu'il les a photographiés, mais pourquoi lui seul les voit-il? Parce qu'il a la grâce.

Il y a ceux qui assènent et ceux qui s'interrogent. Les tenants du point d'exclamation et ceux du point d'interrogation. Or quoi de plus beau, même typographiquement, qu'un point d'interrogation? »La mort et la vulgarité sont les seules choses qu'on ne puisse expliquer« a écrit Oscar Wilde (encore lui!), mais ce n'est qu'un bon mot. On ne peut rien expliquer, même si l'on passe sa vie à tenter de le faire, et la photographie a cette prétention, pour certains, d'expliquer en »montrant objectivement«.

Erreur fatale! La photographie ne montre rien, que des apparences. Tel visage sera triste pour l'un, ennuyé pour l'autre, calme pour un troisième. Chacun apporte à la compréhension d'une image sa propre imagination, ses souvenirs, ses goûts. Evidemment, la photographie d'une maison blanche sera la représentation véridique d'une maison blanche… bien que… avec des filtres… des trucages de laboratoire… bref, il

solche, die sich ihnen stellen: Anhänger des Fragezeichens. Was ist schöner als ein Fragezeichen? »Der Tod und die Banalität sind die einzigen Dinge, die man nicht erklären kann«, schrieb Oscar Wilde (schon wieder er!), doch das ist nur ein Bonmot. Man kann nichts erklären, selbst wenn man es ein Leben lang versucht. Für manche ist die Photographie mit dem Anspruch verbunden, Dinge zu erklären, indem sie sie »objektiv zeigt«.

Welch fataler Irrtum! Die Photographie zeigt nichts als Erscheinungsformen. Dasselbe Gesicht mag für den einen Trauer, für den anderen Langeweile und für einen dritten Ruhe ausstrahlen. Bei jedem Menschen tragen die Phantasie, die Erinnerungen und Neigungen zum Verständnis des Bildes bei. Die Photographie eines weißen Hauses ist natürlich die wahrheitsgetreue Darstellung eines weißen Hauses, wenn auch mit Hilfe von Filtern, Kunstgriffen im Labor und so weiter; kurz, es geht hier weniger um ein Wissen als um ein Nachempfinden.

Die »Vier Jahreszeiten« hatten für Vivaldi bestimmte Farben. Höre ich den »Winter«, sehe ich immer den »Frühling«. Spielt das eine Rolle?

Ließe man bei den Porträts von August Sander die Bildlegenden fort, so würden die Berufe seiner Modelle austauschbar (bis auf den Fleischer vielleicht), ohne daß sie an Qualität verlören. Die »Revolutionäre« könnten ohne weiteres zu »Klavierlehrern« werden, und die »Jungen Bäuerinnen« zu »Städterinnen auf einer Landpartie«, was sie im übrigen vielleicht auch geworden sind.

Natürlich übertreibe ich ein wenig. Eine Photographie besitzt immer einen gewissen Kern Wahrheit und Informationswert. Irving Penns Porträt von Pablo Picasso zeigt natürlich Picasso, und zwar in einem bestimmten Augenblick seines Lebens und so, wie Penn ihn gesehen hat. Doch wissen wir bereits aus anderen Quellen, daß es sich um Picasso handelt. Dasselbe Bild mag für einen tibetani-

Each person brings to his understanding of the image his own imagination, his own memories, his own tastes. Obviously, a photograph of a white house is a true representation of a white house. But, with the right filter, tricks of the laboratory... In short, it's less a question of knowing than of feeling. For Vivaldi, each of the »Four Seasons« had a specific colour. For myself, when I hear »Winter«, I see »Spring«. Does it matter?

If you took away the captions to August Sander's portraits, you could interchange the professions of his models (with the exception, perhaps, of the butcher!) without depriving them of one iota of their worth. The »Revolutionaries« could just as well be the »Piano teachers« and the »Young Peasant Girls« could be the bourgeois matrons on a spree — which they indeed may have become!

I'm obviously exaggerating slightly. A photograph will always have a certain element of truth, of information. Irving Penn's portrait of Pablo Picasso is a good representation of Picasso at a certain moment of his life, such as he appeared to Penn. But we already know, from other sources, that it is Picasso, we know his face, we've seen it in films and in real life. To a Tibetan peasant, the same portait would just be some mean old fellow who maybe reminds him of his grandfather. It is the way of regarding something, the quality of the subject that persist, not information in the strict sense. In fact, the most moving images are often those about which we have no information and which offer us none – an old school photo, found at a jumble sale, anonymous faces, you wonder who they were, what's happened to them, are they still alive?

Too much analysis kills emotion. Rather than didactic photography, I prefer the photography of sentiment where the subject is less important than the way in which it is perceived. There are no good or bad subjects, there's only the way in which they are seen.

s'agit moins de savoir que de ressentir.

Les »Quatre Saisons« avaient chacune une »couleur« spécifique pour Vivaldi. Moi, en entendant l'»Hiver«, je vois le »Printemps«, est-ce important?

Si l'on supprimait les légendes des portraits d'August Sander, on pourrait intervertir les professions de tous ses modèles (sauf le boucher peut-être!) sans que cela enlève une parcelle de leur qualité. Les »Révolutionnaires« pourraient parfaitement devenir »Professeurs de piano«, et les »Jeunes paysannes« des bourgeoises en goguette, ce qu'elles sont d'ailleurs peut-être devenues!

Evidemment, j'exagère un peu. Une photographie aura toujours une certaine part de vérité, d'information. Le portrait de Pablo Picasso par Irving Penn représente bien Picasso à un certain moment de sa vie, tel que Penn l'a ressenti. Mais nous savions déjà, par d'autres sources, qu'il s'agissait de Picasso, parce que nous connaissions son visage, l'ayant vu dans des films, dans la vie. Cette même image, pour un paysan tibétain, ne sera que celle d'un vieillard malicieux qui lui rappellera peut-être son grand-père.

C'est la qualité du regard et du sujet qui subsistera, plus que l'information proprement dite. D'ailleurs, les images les plus émouvantes sont souvent celles dont on ne possède aucune information ou qui ne nous en procurent aucune: une vieille photo de classe trouvée aux Puces, visages anonymes dont on se demande qui ils étaient et ce qu'ils sont devenus, s'ils vivent même encore?

A trop vouloir analyser, on tue l'émotion; à la photographie didactique, je préfère celle du sentiment, celle dans laquelle le sujet importe moins que le regard porté sur lui.

Il n'y a pas de bons ou de mauvais sujets, il n'y a que la qualité du regard qui se pose sur eux.

Je serais assez partisan d'une association, loi de 1901, qui pourrait s'appeler »Laissez-les vivre« (si ce nom

schen Bauern nichts weiter darstellen als einen schelmischen Alten, der ihn vielleicht an seinen Großvater erinnert. Mehr noch als die Information im eigentlichen Sinn überdauern der spezifische Blickwinkel und das Thema.

Häufig bewegen uns die Bilder am stärksten, über die wir nichts wissen: ein altes Klassenphoto, das man auf dem Flohmarkt findet; unbekannte Gesichter, bei denen man sich fragt, wer sie waren, was aus ihnen geworden ist und ob sie noch leben. Wenn man zuviel analysiert, tötet man das Gefühl ab. Ich ziehe der didaktischen Photographie die des Gefühls vor, in der das Sujet weniger wichtig ist als die Sicht, aus der man es sieht. Es gibt keine guten oder schlechten Sujets, es gibt nur die Qualität des Blickwinkels, aus der man sie betrachtet.

Ich würde mich für einen Verein einsetzen, der den Namen »Laissez-les vivre« (»Laßt sie leben«) tragen könnte (wenn dieser Name nicht bereits belegt wäre) und der es sich zum Ziel† setzen würde, die Bilder leben zu lassen und die Exegeten auszuschalten. Das gleiche könnte man übrigens auch für den Film, die Literatur oder die Musik einführen. Vor einigen Jahren wollte ich mit Freunden eine Zeitschrift mit Bildern und Texten herausgeben; der schönste Titel, der mir einfiel, war »Die Stille«. Sie wurde natürlich nie realisiert.

Hintern aus der Zeit nach dem Mai 68

12. Juni 1974: Ein Porträt zu machen bedeutet meist, daß man ein Gesicht oder eine Büste in einer vertrauten oder neutralen Umgebung darstellt. Das Gesicht ist der exponierteste Teil des Körpers, der Teil, der am besten zu sehen ist und im sozialen Leben am meisten Verwendung findet. Es ist zur heuchlerischen

I would be in favour of an association, from the law of 1901, calling itself »Let them be«, (if the name hadn't already been taken! – »Laissez-les vivre«) whose function would be to get rid of the interpreters and let images speak for themselves. One could in fact do the same thing for cinema, literature and music.

A few years ago, we wanted, with a few friends, to start a journal which would consist of text and images. The best title I could thing of was »Silence«. Naturally, it was never to be!

Derrières after May 68

12 June 1974: Very often, a portrait consists of showing a face or bust in a familiar or neutral setting. The face is, of course, the most exposed part of the body, the most visible, the part most utilised in social life. But it has become a hypocritical mask which can be made to express anything one wants, to laugh when one is sad, to appear interested when one is dying of boredom, to be as marble when one is burning with passion.

This is one of the reasons why I became interested in derrières. It is, in effect, the most protected part of the body, the most secret, the part which preserves its childlike innocence when face and hands have long since lost theirs. From an artistic point of view, it's also the most moving part of the body (in the female form that is!), composed of curves and promises. It's the part which remembers, which looks towards the past while we

n'était déja usurpé!) et dont le but serait de laisser vivre les images en en supprimant les exégètes. On pourrait d'ailleurs faire la même chose pour le cinéma, la littérature ou la musique. Il y a quelques années nous voulions, avec des amis, faire une revue d'images et de textes, et le plus beau titre que j'avais trouvé était »le Silence«. Elle n'a évidemment jamais vu le jour!

Derrières postérieurs »à mai 68«

12 Juin 1974: Faire un portrait consiste, le plus souvent, à représenter un visage ou un buste dans un environnement familier ou neutre. Or, le visage est la partie du corps qui est la plus exposée, la plus utilisée dans la vie sociale. Il est devenu ce masque hypocrite auquel on peut faire exprimer ce que l'on veut, qui peut rire lorsqu'on est triste, paraître intéressé lorsqu'on meurt d'ennui, être de marbre quand on bouillonne de passion.

C'est une des raisons pour lesquelles j'ai commencé à m'intéresser aux derrières. C'est en effet la partie la plus protégée, la plus secrète, celle qui conserve cette innocence enfantine que le regard ou les mains ont depuis longtemps perdue. C'est, aussi, la partie du corps, plastiquement, la plus émouvante (chez les dames s'entend!), faite de rondeurs et de promesses; c'est elle qui se souvient, qui est tournée vers le passé alors que nous allons inexorablement de l'avant, et qui regarde le chemin parcouru, commes les enfants accoudés à la lunette arrière d'une voiture et rêvant à la route qui défile sans se préoccuper de la destination du voyage.

Les derrières sont aussi divers que le sont les individus: il en est de purement fonctionnnels, qui ne servent

Maske geworden, mit der man ausdrücken kann, was man will: die lachen kann, wenn man traurig ist, interessiert erscheinen kann, wenn man sich zu Tode langweilt, und steinern erscheinen kann, wenn im Innern die Leidenschaft brodelt.

Das ist einer der Gründe, weshalb ich begonnen habe, mich für Hinterteile zu interessieren. Denn der Hintern ist der bestgeschützte Teil des Körpers, der verborgenste, der zudem die kindliche Unschuld bewahrt, die die Augen oder die Hände seit langem verloren haben. Plastisch gesehen ist er zudem der bewegendste Teil (bei den Damen, versteht sich), bestehend aus Rundungen und Verheißungen. Er erinnert sich, ist der Vergangenheit zugewandt, während wir unerbittlich vorwärtsgehen; er richtet den Blick auf den zurückgelegten Weg wie die Kinder, die im Auto mit aufgestützten Ellbogen zur Heckscheibe hinausschauen und träumend der dahinziehenden Straße nachhängen, ohne sich um das Ziel der Reise zu kümmern.

Die Hintern sind ebenso unterschiedlich wie die Menschen. Es gibt rein funktionelle, die zu nichts anderem dienen, als sich hinzusetzen oder zu kacken. Solche Hintern sind uninteressant und den Gesichtern ihrer Besitzer häufig nur allzu ähnlich. Andere sind einfach neutral, geschlechtslos, möchte ich behaupten, kurz: langweilig. Und schließlich gibt es die außergewöhnlichen, eleganten, aristokratischen Hintern, die über ihre Funktion hinauswachsen, sie sublimieren, zu Kunstwerken werden, zu Meisterwerken, zu Wunderwerken der Natur. Das sind die romanischen Gewölbe der Körperarchitektur, die den ursprünglichen Glauben an die Frau als das Ebenbild Gottes wiederfinden lassen. Solche Hintern photographiere ich gerne, um ihre wunderbaren Kurven für immer festzuhalten, bevor die Zeit sie vergehen läßt. Diese Hintern hätten es beinahe verdient – als höchste Auszeichnung für ihre Einzigartigkeit –, kein Arschloch zu haben.

move inexorably forward. It looks back along the way we have travelled, like children looking out the rear window of a car and dreamily watching the road disappear, with no thought for the journey's destination. There are as many derrières as there are people. There are those which are purely functional, which can only be used for sitting or shitting; these are without interest and resemble only too clearly the faces of their owners. Others are simply neutral, asexual one might say, in short, dull. Then there are the rare ones, elegant, aristocratic, which surpass their function, sublimate, become works of art, masterpieces, miracles of nature. Romanesque vaults of bodily architecture, these women made in God's image lead one to rediscover original faith. These are the ones I like to photograph, to conserve for ever the miraculous curves before time has a chance to destroy them. These derrières almost deserve the ultimate accolade for their uniqueness: to have no ass-hole.

qu'à s'asseoir au à faire caca, ceux-là ne sont pas intéressants et ressemblent souvent par trop aux visages de leurs propriétaires. D'autres sont simplement neutres, asexués oserais-je dire … bref, ennuyeux. Enfin, il y a les derrières rares, élégants, aristocratiques, qui dépassent leur fonction, la subliment, deviennent objets d'art, chefs-d'œuvre, miracles de la nature. Ce sont les voûtes romanes de l'architecture corporelle, qui permettent de retrouver la foi originelle en une Femme à l'image de Dieu. Ce sont ceux-là que j'aime photographier, pour en conserver à jamais les courbes miraculeuses avant que le temps ne les dégrade. Ces derrières-là mériteraient presque, récompense ultime de leur unicité, de n'avoir point de trou du cul.

Niemand gelangt auf Anhieb zur Frivolität.
Sie ist ein Privileg und eine Kunst.

No one acquires frivolity straight away.
It is a privilege and an art.

Personne n'atteint d'emblée la frivolité.
C'est un privilège et un art.

Und wenn es einen Bereich gibt, in dem jeder allein ist,
dann gewiß den der Lust und der Phantasie.

If there's one area in which we are truly alone,
it is that of our sensual pleasure and fantasy.

S'il est un domaine où chacun est solitaire,
c'est bien celui du plaisir et des phantasmes…

Ein Bild ist, um wirkungsvoll zu sein, in gewisser Weise
dazu verurteilt, »schön« zu sein.

An image has to be »beautiful« to be
effective.

Une image est, d'une certain façon, condamnée à
être »belle« pour être efficace.

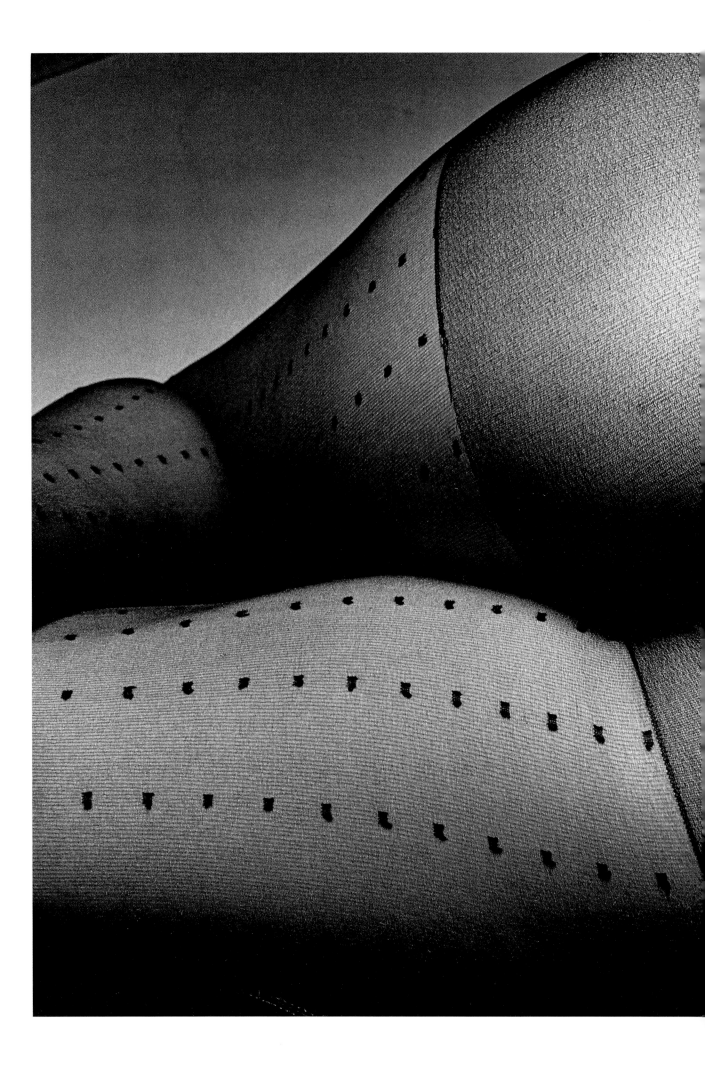

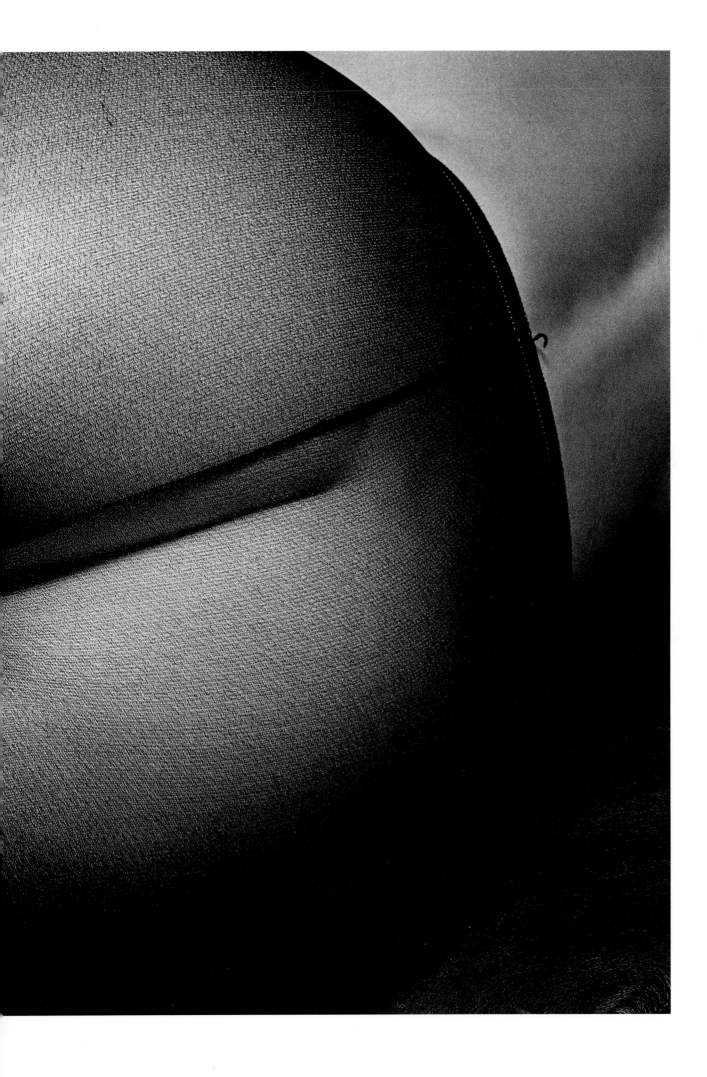

Ich wollte die Zeit im glorreichen Moment der Jugend
anhalten und den Inbegriff von Jugend dargestellt wissen.

I wanted to stop the progress of time at the glorious
moment of youth and portray the essence of youth.

Je voulais arrêter le temps à ce moment glorieux de la
jeunesse pour avoir la certitude d'en avoir representé la
quintessence.

Meine Bilder sind imaginäre Erinnerungen, in einem
durchsichtigen Spiegel gesehen.

My images are imaginary memories seen through
a two-way mirror.

Mes images sont des souvenirs imaginaires vus dans un
miroir sans tain.

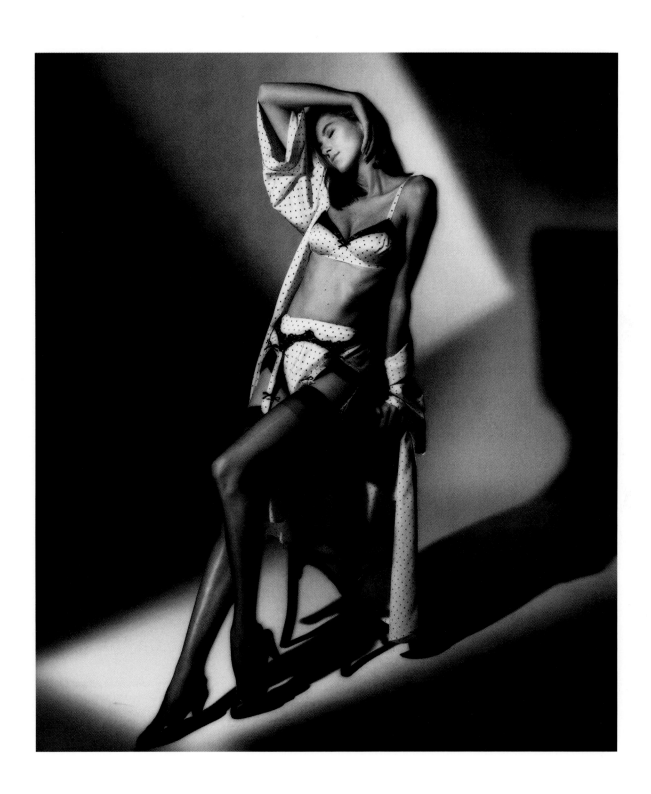

Es handelt sich mit anderen Worten um ganz normale
junge Mädchen und Frauen, die oft nur das eine
miteinander verbindet: in relativ kurzer Zeit durch die
Vermarktung ihrer Figur zu Geld zu kommen.

In other words, these are quite ordinary young girls
and women linked solely by one thing:
earning easy money by marketing their figure.

En d'autres mots, il s'agit de jeune filles ou de jeunes
femmes, qui, souvent, n'ont qu'une chose en commun:
tirer profit de leur corps pour gagner de l'argent en
relativement peu de temps.

Es gibt keine guten oder schlechten Sujets, es gibt nur die
Qualität des Blickwinkels, aus der man sie betrachtet.

There are no good or bad subjects, there's
only the way in which they are seen.

Il n'y a pas de bons ou de mauvais sujets, il n'y a que la
qualité du regard qui se pose sur eux.

Biographie

1933 wurde Jeanloup Sieff als Sohn polnischstämmiger Eltern in Paris geboren.

1945–1954 besuchte er die Gymnasien Chaptal und Decours. Nach dem Abitur studierte er kurze Zeit Literaturwissenschaft (zwei Wochen), Journalismus (zehn Tage) und Photographie an der Schule Vaugirard/Frankreich (einen Monat) und in Vevey/Schweiz (sieben Monate). Zuvor hatte er sehr kurze Zeit in Betracht gezogen, am IDHEC (Institut des Hautes Etudes Cinématographiques) Regie zu studieren. Bereits seit seinem fünfzehnten Lebensjahr war er als Amateurphotograph tätig.

1954 gab er seine ersten »professionellen« Debüts mit Reportagen.

1955–1958 arbeitete er für die Zeitschrift *Elle* – zunächst mit Reportagen, dann im Bereich Mode.

1959–1961 arbeitete er für *Réalités, Le Jardin des Mode*. Er trennte sich von der Agentur *Magnum*, um unabhängig arbeiten zu können. 1959 erhielt er den Prix Niepce.

1961–1965 lebte und arbeitete er in New York; Beiträge u.a. für die Zeitschriften *Look, Esquire* und vor allem für *Harper's Bazaar*. Zwischenaufenthalte in Europa mit Beiträgen für *Twen, Vogue, Queen*.

Seit 1967 lebt und arbeitet er wieder in Paris. Regelmäßige Beiträge für *Vogue, Femme, Nova* und andere Zeitschriften. Er arbeitet an Büchern, Beiträgen für Radio und Fernsehen und anderem mehr. Seine Photographien wurden auf zahlreichen nationalen und internationalen Gruppen- und Einzelausstellungen gezeigt und von Museen angekauft. Seine letzte große Ausstellung, eine Retrospektive, hatte er in Paris im Musée d'Art Moderne (Mai–September 1986).

Biography

1933 Jeanloup Sieff was born in Paris to parents of Polish extraction.

1945–1954 general education at the Chaptal and Decours grammar schools, then brief study of literature (two weeks), journalism (ten days) and photography at the Vaugirard School (one month) and in Vevey, Switzerland (seven months) – considered film production at the IDHEC (Institut des Hautes Etudes Cinématographiques). Began amateur photography at the age of fourteen.

1954 first »professional« works for the press.

1955–1958 working for the magazine *Elle*, firstly with the news department then in the fashion section.

1959–1961 working for *Réalités, Le Jardin des Modes*. Left the *Magnum* agency to continue working freelance. Received the Prix Niepce.

1961–1965 living and working in New York; photographic works for the magazines *Look, Esquire* and, above all, *Harper's Bazaar*. During extended trips to Europe contributions also to *Twen, Vogue* and *Queen*.

Since 1967 living and working in Paris again. Regular contributions to *Vogue, Femme, Nova* and other magazines. Sieff has worked on various books, radio and television programmes and many other projects. His photographs have been displayed at numerous national and international exhibitions and bought by museums. His last exhibition, a broad retrospective view of his works, was given at the Musée d'Art Moderne in Paris (May–September 1986).

Biographie

1933 Naissance à Paris de parents d'origine polonaise.

1945–1954 Etudes secondaires au lycée Chaptal et Decours. Après le bac, brèves études de lettres (deux semaines), de journalisme (dix jours), de photographie à l'école Vaugirard/France (un mois) et à Vevey/Suisse (sept mois). Avait envisagé d'étudier la mise en scène à l'Institut des Hautes Etudes Cinématographiques. Pratique la photo en amateur depuis l'âge de quinze ans.

1954 Débuts de photographe-journaliste.

1955–1958 Engagé par le journal *Elle*, d'abord comme reporter-photographe, puis comme photographe de mode.

1959–1961 Travaille pour les revues *Réalités* et *Le Jardin des Modes*. Quitte l'agence »Magnum« pour pouvoir être indépendant. Obtient le prix Niepce en 1959.

1961–1965 Vit et travaille à New York. Collabore à *Look, Esquire*, et surtout *Harper's Bazaar*. Courts séjours en Europe pendant lesquels il travaille pour *Twen, Vogue* et *Queen*.

Depuis 1967 Vit et travaille à Paris. Collaboration régulière avec *Vogue, Femme, Nova* ainsi qu'avec d'autres magazines. Travaille par ailleurs à des livres, participe à des émissions de radio ou de télé. Objets d'expositions nationales et internationales, ses photos ont été achetées par de nombreux musées. Le Musée d'Art Moderne a organisé récemment une grande rétrospective de ses œuvres de mai à septembre 1986.

Bildlegenden/Captions/Légendes

P. 14:   Fetischismus/Fetishism/
Fétichisme, 1985

P. 15:   Fetischismus/Fetishism/Féti-
chisme, 1985

P. 16:   Hintern in der Sonne/Bottom
in der Sonne/Derrière au soleil, Paris
1981

P. 17:   Hintern in der Sonne/Bottom
in the sun/Derrière au soleil, Paris
1984

P. 18:   Kleid von J. M. Sinan/Dress
by J. M. Sinan/Robe de J. M. Sinan,
Paris 1987

P. 19:   Kleid von Azzedine Alaïa/
Dress by Azzedine Alaïa/Robe
d'Azzedine Alaïa, 1986

P. 20:   Fetischismus/Fetishism/Féti-
chisme, 1987

P. 21:   Fetischismus/Fetishism/Féti-
chisme, 1987

P. 22:   Modephoto/Fashion photo/
Photo de mode, Paris 1978

P. 23:   Dessous/Lingerie, 1986

P. 25:   Sappho/Sapho, 1974

P. 26:   Schuhe/Shoes/Chaussures,
1986

P. 27:   Frau mit Schleier/Woman
with a veil/Femme avec voilette,
Paris 1985

P. 28:   Frauenakt in einer Biblio-
thek/Naked woman in a library/
Femme nue dans une bibliothèque,
1976

P. 29:   Dessous/Lingerie, 1983

P. 30:   Lolita für *Vogue*/Lolita for
Vogue/Lolita pour *Vogue*, Paris 1980

P. 31:   Modephoto/Fashion photo/
Photo de mode, 1983

P. 33:   Wache, nackte Frau auf
einem Kanapee/Naked woman
awake on a sofa/Femme nue,
éveillée, sur un canapé, 1974

P. 34:   Porträt einer sitzenden
Dame/Portrait of a woman sitting/
Portrait d'une dame assise, 1972

P. 35:   Modephoto/Fashion photo/
Photo de mode, Paris 1978

P. 36:   Modephoto/Fashion photo/
Photo de mode, 1987

P. 37:   Schwarzes Kleid/Black
dress/Robe noire, Paris 1986

P. 38:   Schwarzes Kleid/Black
dress/Robe noire, Paris 1986

P. 39:   Frau unter einem Auto,
offene Haube/Woman under a car,
bonnet up/Seule sous une voiture,
capots ouverts, Paris 1975

P. 41:   Dessous/Lingerie, 1985

P. 42:   Fetischismus/Fetishism/Féti-
chisme, Paris 1985

P. 43:   Modephoto/Fashion photo/
Photo de mode, 1979

P. 44:   Hüte/Hats/Chapeaux, 1986

P. 45:   Kleid von Yves Saint Laurent
für *Vogue*/Dress by Yves Saint Laurent for *Vogue*/Robe d'Yves Saint
Laurent pour *Vogue*, Paris 1970

P. 46/47:   Hintern in einer Strumpf-
hose/Bottom in tights/Derrière,
dans un collant, 1981

P. 48:   Dessous/Lingerie, 1986

P. 49:   Dessous/Lingerie, 1986

P. 50:   Nackte Frau auf einem
gestreiften Bett/Naked woman on a
striped bed/Femme nue sur un lit
rayé, Paris 1975

P. 51:   Akt in einem Spiegel/Nude in
a mirror/Nu dans un miroir, Paris
1976

P. 53:   Charlotte Rampling, 1985

P. 54:   »Torses Nus«: Midori, 1986

P. 55:   »Torses Nus«, Tierney, 1986

P. 56:   Werbephoto für Schuhe/
Advertisement for shoes/Publicité
pour chaussures, 1985

P. 57:   Gestreiftes Abendkleid/
Striped evening dress/Robe rayée,
1985

P. 58:   Dessous/Lingerie, 1986

P. 59:   Dessous/Lingerie, 1986

P. 61:   Akt auf einer Treppe/Nude
on the stairs/Nu dans un escalier,
Paris 1987

P. 62:   Cristelle, Paris 1987

P. 63:   Dessous/Lingerie, Paris 1988

P. 64:   Isabelle, Paris 1987

P. 65:   Dessous aus Baumwolle/
Cotton lingerie/Lingerie de coton,
1987

P. 66:   Akt mit Zopf/Nude with
plait/Nu avec natte, Paris 1985

P. 67:   Dessous/Lingerie, 1987

P. 68:   Modephoto für *Vogue*/
Fashion photo for *Vogue*/Photo de
mode pour *Vogue*, Paris 1984

P. 69:   Es lebe Frankreich/Vive la
France, Paris 1984

P. 70:   Werbephoto für Strümpfe/
Advertisement for stockings/Publi-
cité pour des collants, 1988

P. 71:   Werbephoto für Strümpfe/
Advertisement for stockings/Publi-
cité pour des collants, 1988

P. 73:   Modephoto/Fashion photo/
Photo de mode, 1981

P. 74:   Auf einem Bett liegend/
Lying on a bed/Bas sur un lit, Paris
1987

P. 75:   Akt auf einem Sofa/Nude on
a sofa/Nu sur canapé, Paris 1987

P. 76:   »Chic is« für *Harper's Ba-
zaar*/»Chic is« for *Harper's Bazaar*/
»Chic is« pour *Harper's Bazaar*,
Palm Beach 1964

Bibliographie/Bibliography

**Monographien/Monographs
Monographies**

J'aime la danse. Texte de Jean Laurent.
Ed. Recontre, Lausanne 1962

La Photo, avec Chenz. Ed. Denoël, Paris
1976 et 1985

La Vallée de la Mort. Texte et Photos
Jeanloup Sieff. Ed. Denoël, Paris 1978;
Schirmer/Mosel, München 1979

Best of Nudes. Tokyo 1980

Portraits de Dames assises… Ed.
Contrejour, Paris 1982; Schirmer/Mosel,
München 1982

Jeanloup Sieff. Monographie dans la
Collection »I grandi fotographi«. Fabbri,
Milan 1982; Filipacchi, Paris 1983

Vers les Cieux d'Or. Illustration du
journal de voyage de Guy de Maupassant en Sicile. Ed. Novecento, Palermo
1984

Torses Nus. Texte et Photos: Jeanloup
Sieff. Ed. Contrejour, Paris 1986;
Schirmer/Mosel, München 1986

Borinage 1959. Essai sur les grèves de
mineurs en Belgique. Musée de la
Photographie, Charleroi/Belgique 1986

Jeanloup Sieff. Monographie. Ed. Parco,
Tokyo 1987

**Sammelbände (Auswahl)
Anthologies (selected)
Livres de Groupe (sélection)**

Masterpiece of Erotic Photography.
Talisman Books, London 1977

Contact-Theory. Lustrum, New York 1980

Le Nu Français. Ed. Jannick, Paris 1983

Private Viewing. Ed. Terry Jones,
London 1983

Carte blanche à…, Angenieux. Ed.
Contrejour, Paris 1984

Marne la Vallée. Ed. Beba, Paris 1987

Nude. Asahi Shuppan, Tokyo 1987

**Kataloge und Portfolios
(Auswahl)/Catalogues and
Portfolios/(selected) Catalogues
et Portfolios (sélection)**

Coffret 12 reproductions. Musée de
Gand 1972

Coffret 12 reproductions *Intimode,*
Ed. Safronoff, Paris 1983

Catalogue: Galerie La Demeure,
J. P. Sudre, Paris 1967

Catalogue: Galerie »Château d'eau«,
Toulouse 1982

Catalogue: Musée d'Art Moderne,
textes de F. Nourissier, F. Marquet et
C. Nori, Paris 1986

Posterbook *Jeanloup Sieff,* Taco,
Berlin 1989

**Buchprojekte/Bookprojects
Projets de Livres**

Derrières. Hommage à 127 derrières
choisis pour leur qualités
plastiques, intellectuelles ou
morales.

Au Nord du Nord. Journal de voyage
en Islande.

Le Monsieur Gris. Roman
commencé en 1974 mais qui ne sera
probablement jamais terminé!

Forbidden Dreams. Benedikt
Taschen Verlag

Ausstellungen/Exhibitions/Expositions

**Einzelausstellungen/Solo exhibitions
Expositions particulières**

1969 Galerie la Demeure, Paris

1970 Wanderausstellung/Travelling exhibition/Exposition personnelle itinérante: Maison de la Culture d'Amiens, Angers, Tours, Le Havre

1971 Underground Gallery, New York
Académie d'Art Moderne, Gand
Wanderausstellung/Travelling exhibition/Exposition itinérante: Maisons de la Culture d'Abbeville, Bordeaux

1972 Galerie Nikon, Paris

1973 Galerie des Philosophes, Genève
Nikon Gallery, Tokyo

1974 Spectrum Gallery, Barcelona

1975 Canon Gallery, Amsterdam
Silver Image, Tacoma (USA)
FNAC Montparnasse, Paris

1976 Galerie Agathe Gaillard, Paris, *43 portraits de Dames remarquables pour une raison ou une autre, dont quelques paysages hautains*
Foster White Gallery, Seattle

Galerie Dieuzaide, Toulouse

1977 Galerie Paule Pia, Anvers

1978 Photogalerie Portfolio, Lausanne
Libraire la Hune, Paris

1979 Fiolet Gallery, Amsterdam

1981 Galerie Netzhaut, Frankfurt

1982 Silver Vision Gallery, Tulsa (USA)
Watari Gallery, Tokyo
FNAC Montparnasse, Mois de la Photo, Paris
Galerie municipale »Le Château d'eau«, Toulouse
Photogramme Gallery, Montreal
Canon Gallery, Amsterdam
Novecento Gallery, Palermo

1983 Institut français de Cologne, Köln
Hamilton Gallery, London
Osthaus Museum, Hagen

1984 Institut français, Aachen
Centre culturel français, Essen
Festival de Trégor
Festival de Rennes

1985 Wiener Festspiele, Wien

1986 Hamilton Gallery, London

1986 Paris, Musée d'Art Moderne, *Retrospective*
Journées Internationales de la Photo, Montpellier
Musée Nicephore Niepce, Chalon-sur-Saône, *»Torses nus«*

1987 Montreal, *Athènes*

1988 Parco Gallery, Tokyo
Bruxelles, *Botanique*

Gruppenausstellungen/Group exhibitions/Expositions de groupe

1966 *Photographies de mode*, Photokina, Köln

1967 *La jeune photographie française*, Bibliothèque nationale, Paris

1968 Musée Catine, Marseille

1972 *La photographie française*, Warsaw and Moscow

1973 *Confrontation 73*, Université de Dijon

1976 Portfolio 76, Galerie Portfolio, Lausanne
The Human Image, Museum of Art, Washington University
Galerie Canon, Genève

1977 *History of fashion photography*, Rochester (USA)

1979 *La photographie de mode française*, Galerie Zabriskye, Paris

1980 Centre Georges Pompidou, *Instantanés*, Paris

1981 Photoscopie 81, *Essai sur Carolyn Carlson*, Centre national d'art contemporain, Paris
Paris-Paris, Centre Georges Pompidou, Paris

1982 *Photographic de mode – Vogue 1920–1980*, Musée Jacquemart André, Paris
Bibliothèque nationale, Paris

1983 *La photo française*, Buenos Aires

1984 *Photo française: 10 photographes*, Ministère des Relations extérieures, Association Française d'Action Artistique, Sweden, Denmark, Finland

1984 *Regards sur l'architecture*, Angers

1985 *La photographie de mode*, Victoria and Albert Museum, London

1988 Festival d'Arles, Arles